MAKE IT

Happen

MAKE IT
Happen

manifest joy and peace
in the life of your dreams

JOANNE GREGORY

CICO BOOKS

LONDON NEW YORK

Published in 2022 by CICO Books
An imprint of Ryland Peters & Small Ltd
20–21 Jockey's Fields   341 E 116th St
London WC1R 4BW   New York, NY 10029

www.rylandpeters.com

10 9 8 7 6 5 4 3 2 1

A CIP catalog record for this book is available from the
Library of Congress and the British Library.

ISBN: 978 1 80065 122 7

Printed in China

Illustration: Eleanor Carter
Design: Allan Sommerville

In-house editor: Jenny Dye
Senior commissioning editor: Carmel Edmonds
Art director: Sally Powell
Creative director: Leslie Harrington
Head of production: Patricia Harrington
Publishing manager: Penny Craig

Contents

Introduction

Is there something missing in your life? What do you really want? Would you like more money, a new home, new job, new love, or just to be happier? What if I told you that you could have anything you want, and you have the power within you to create it?

Well, you can create what you wish for. Being happy is your birthright. The universe is constructed so that once a clear request is sent out, the laws of the universe are instigated, and a result is guaranteed. A few simple guidelines have to be adhered to, and then anything is possible!

This book guides you through the process of manifestation, which can bring all you desire into your life. It is filled with powerful tools for self-improvement which, when implemented, give you the knowledge to create the life you dream of.

The energy that flows through everything flows through us, so we are linked to everything and everyone—we are an intrinsic part of the universe. And no matter how much or how little we know or remember this, we can all recognize and activate the universe's laws and creative forces. As human beings, we are already equipped with everything we need, but working with intention-focusing techniques will get the process moving and help you reach your potential more quickly.

All you need to do is ask—and it will happen.

CHAPTER ONE

What is
manifestation?

How does the manifestation process work?

We were each born with a special gift. This gift is our imagination—the ability to create something from nothing.

Its impact is evident all around us. Someone, somewhere has an idea or notion and, with a little effort, puts the idea into practice, creating something tangible. From the light bulb to the steam engine, everything is born of an idea, a thought, which manifests these great inventions and discoveries. And this same process can be applied to anything we might want or need in our daily lives. Whether it's a new car or a cure for illness, the system is the same; the manifestation process begins with a single thought or idea. This thought may have been planted in us by the universe at just the right time, or may have lain dormant within us from before birth, just waiting to be awakened at the right moment. Either way, it only takes one thought to start the process.

A thought is given energy depending on how often it is used. The more we think a certain thought, the more energy we give it. It attracts other energies vibrating on the same or similar frequency according to its strength and nature (for instance, how much time the creator has spent thinking about it, and whether it has a positive or negative vibration). These other energies give the creator some kind of feedback about the potential outcome of the thought.

It only takes one
thought to start
the process.

For example, the creator might become aware of a similar experiment or breakthrough, or be offered help by another creator. This is synchronicity at work—when the right information comes just at the right time.

Fuelled by the confirmation that they are on the right track, the creator gives the thought or idea a great deal of thinking time. S/he imagines the outcome in different scenarios, but always imagines success. Related feelings fuel and drive the creator. The energy around the thought is now so vast, and the thought itself is so huge, that it is now more of a "belief." We base our beliefs on things that appear real to us: that is, things we can see and hear, or are told over and over again.

For example, you believe that grass is green, but who says so? Someone, somewhere, in the beginning, made a decision that the color of grass would be called green. You might think this is a silly thing to say, but the point I'm making is we can believe things to be true just because we've been told enough times that they are. (After all, it may be possible that when I see green it is different to what you see.) The vibration then matches the belief and it becomes a reality. Every possible matching vibration is attracted to it, and the desired result is achieved. The thought or idea has become solid; we have fixed our attention on random subatomic particles and set them into the pattern we expected to achieve.

Special manifestation guidelines

So, now you know that you can ask the universe for what you want, how do you do it?

• When you make a request to the universe, be clear. Say it repeatedly, visualize it, affirm it, think it, write it down, pray for it, or meditate on it, or do all of the above. Quite simply, the more energy or attention you give to your request, the more quickly it will be presented to you.

• Learn to think and act like the universe. You will understand why this is important when you consider how time-consuming it is to get a point across to a foreigner when neither of you has any understanding of each other's language. Sometimes it's possible, but it takes so long and there is much room for misinterpretation. Learn to speak the lingo and the problem is removed. The more you practice asking the universe for help, the better you will learn how to speak in the language the universe understands (see page 68).

• Ask from a "feelgood" place. To communicate easily with the universe—and therefore the highest of vibrations—we have to be vibrating as highly as possible ourselves, so when you are thinking about asking the cosmos for help, there is a frequency variation to take into consideration. You need to ask for help from a "feelgood" place. Many of the messages from the universe in this book will help educate you about its frequency (see pages 42, 46, 50, and 113).

Just begin

Why not give manifestation a go?

Decide what it is you want.

You don't have to decide on something forever, just decide what would be nice for now. You can adjust your request at any time.

Write down your wish.

Then tell yourself over again that it's already here. Speaking in the present tense takes your request out of your future and puts it into your present.

Visualize it over and over again.
Start off by feeling a buzz if you can; get to a "feel-good"
place and request from there.

**Read through the messages in this book and see which
one resonates most with you regarding your wish.**
Or open the book at a random page and apply the message to
your wish. Repeat this as often as you like. Believe your request
will come to you, and it will.

**Keep your list of wishes in a safe place or write them down
in the back of this book (see page 124).**
This will allow you to go back to it and tick off requests
as they happen.

CHAPTER TWO

Messages from the universe

Anything is possible

Are you a limited or limitless person? Whatever your answer to this question, you were created limitless.

You are an important part of the intelligent energy that created our entire universe. However we label this energy—maybe God, love, unconditional love—the majority of us believe that there's something out there, and that it is capable of immeasurable greatness. And it follows that if this energy, this source of "all that is," is limitless and we are part of it, we too have no limits. This energy, the universe, and its inhabitants are all part of one magnificent whole. We are so closely connected that the evolution of each of us has a direct impact on the evolution of the whole of our species.

Physicists can prove that what we believe to be true becomes real for us. A common quantum experiment to monitor the behavior of atoms, called the dual slit experiment, proves that we have an effect on how atoms behave. The outcome of the experiment is dependent on the belief system of the observer (the person carrying out the experiment). Atoms are the building blocks of the universe, and concentrating on them affects how they behave; so for you, whatever you concentrate on can manifest in your life.

Anything is possible!

Embrace the notion that you have
no limitations and that no goal is out
of reach. The only thing that prevents
you from bringing all you desire to you
is what you believe. Whatever
you believe to be true will be!

Think about what you say

Thoughts are very real, measurable things. The effects of thought waves and sound waves on our environment, elements, and each other can be scientifically validated.

Author and researcher Dr. Masaru Emoto carried out a series of enlightening experiments with water droplets. Vials of ordinary mineral water had positive and negative words attached to them, then a drop of water from each vial was frozen on a slide. The water labeled with positive affirmations made beautiful snowflake-like ice crystals, but the negatively-labeled water crystals were jagged and dark.

Given that we are made up of at least 70 percent water, we can see that thoughts and words are very powerful tools, and the positive or negative vibrations connected with them can have a phenomenal effect. For the most part, this is common sense; unkind words hurt, whereas kind words lift your vibration and make you feel good.

Be selective about the words you choose, and give little or no energy, through thought, to negative words and situations to avoid helping them grow. When you think positively, you are also evoking the law of attraction—like attracts like. Try thinking that helpful people surround you and that you are loved, and watch those people turn up!

Remember that like attracts like. The more you fill your day with positive energy, the more positive energy will come to you, bringing great things with it. Negative people and situations cannot exist in a world filled with positive energy.

What goes around comes around

This is an old but essential adage; what we send out, we receive.

From the seventeenth century, scientists have been looking into entrainment, also known as synchronicity or resonance, which is defined as the tendency for two oscillating bodies to lock into phase so that they vibrate in harmony.

During a seminar run by author and researcher Lynne McTaggart, I witnessed an experiment on two men residing in different continents. One man sent positive thoughts to the other while their vital signs were monitored. From that second, both men began to resonate at the same frequency—their heart rates and brain activities quickly synchronized.

Remember that what you send out into the universe will affect you first and foremost. Revenge-based requests will only hurt you, while love-based ones will empower you both.

This indicates that our thoughts affect others and return to affect us, too. On every level, we get back what we send out. Within the universe there is a perfect balance, or karma—a payment for how you live your life. How you behave creates your individual karma. If you do a good deed just when it is needed, someone will do something good for you. It may not be the person you originally helped who balances the transaction, but it always gets balanced. It is the same when someone hurts you. You may not be around to see their karma balanced out, but it will happen.

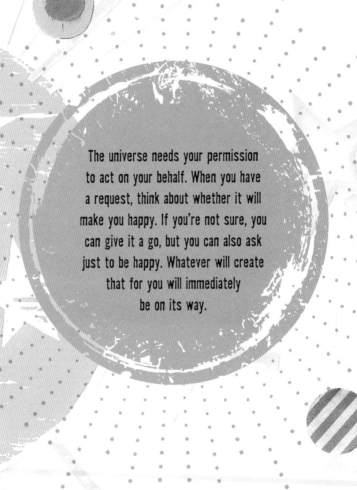

The universe needs your permission
to act on your behalf. When you have
a request, think about whether it will
make you happy. If you're not sure, you
can give it a go, but you can also ask
just to be happy. Whatever will create
that for you will immediately
be on its way.

You can ask for help

**The life we lead is our own doing; no one else is to blame
or can take credit for what we see before us.**

The reason for this is that we were born with free will. It is the best and
probably only way in which we can truly learn. Free will gives us choice
about how we behave and react to what happens to us. The final
decision is always our own.

How many toddlers will still touch something hot, despite the warnings
from doting parents? And how many will touch something hot again
after experiencing the pain of a burn? We learn best from experience.

Because of free will, the universe cannot act on our behalf without our
permission. It just waits patiently for a request and then gets to work on
whatever it is we repeatedly send out to it, whether good or bad. It may
know what is best for us and know how we should avoid all the pitfalls,
but the universe cannot guide us unless we say it is okay to do so.
If your life is less than you would like it to be, change begins with
a clear request. Ask and it will happen!

Say what you want

One of the most effective ways to achieve your dream is by affirming clearly, as many times as possible, what you want with words and thoughts.

You can think about your requests and/or say them out loud repeatedly to yourself or anyone else that might care to listen. The more energy you invest, the stronger the affirmation becomes, and the more you say something, the quicker the return.

Try the following ways to double the power of your request:

- Write down your affirmation and read it periodically.

- Print out your affirmation and display it around your home or place of work.

- Stick notes containing affirmations near your computer, and also on the refrigerator and mirrors in your home, to remind you of your intent. My family and I like to do this—when more than one person uses the same affirmation for a common goal, the results can be mind-blowing.

Say what it is you want. Step up your affirmations and vocalize your wish at every possible opportunity.

Spend time thinking about what it is you really want. Is your wish hiding another wish below it? Why not peel back the layers? You may discover that all you want is to be happy or feel alive! In which case, just ask and it will happen.

Know what it is you want

Knowing what you want is half the battle. If you are really unsure of what you want, you can start with what you don't want and work from there.

When you do decide, spend time thinking it through and be specific, for example:

- If it's the man or woman of your dreams, muse on what color hair and eyes they might have.

- If it's a new job, what are the ideal hours and salary?

- If it's a new home, where will it be and what will it look like?

The more detail you can give, the more accurate your manifestation.

Sometimes all we need to ask for is peace and happiness, and everything that we desire will come to us with it. We don't always know what will make us happy; how many times have you bought something and then changed your mind about it?

Also, consider this: is your wish hiding another wish? Ask yourself exactly why you want another job. Is it to earn more money? And if you want more money, is it so that you can buy nice things? Then think: what will the nice things do when they're here? Make me happy? If so, simply ask the universe for happiness, rather than the job.

Say it now—in the present tense

Affirmations are more effective when they are voiced in the present tense. Time is a man-made tool created to give order to our lives, and it is present in this dimension only.

Thanks to Einstein's theory of relativity, we know that if we could travel at the speed of light, time would stop for us because photons of light don't age. If time did not exist, the only moment that would be relevant is this one.

The majority of the unseen universe vibrates on a frequency equal to or above the speed of light and so is not restricted by time, particularly the part that helps us manifest our dreams. Present-tense affirmations are therefore more powerful. For example:

"I am debt-free," as opposed to: **"I am going to be debt-free."**
Or, better yet: **"I have all the money I need to pay off my bills and more besides to buy the things I want."**

"My soul mate is in my life," as opposed to:
"I am going to find my soul mate."

"I feel fulfilled in my career," as opposed to:
"I am going to find a career I love."

To imply that are you going to have or do or be something puts it into the future tense and, after all, it has been said that tomorrow never comes.

Remember that only a small percentage
of the universe is under the influence of time.
Voicing all your affirmations as if they have
already happened, or are happening, makes
them real in the present moment and helps
your wishes manifest more quickly.

Be patient

Due to the way the dimension in which we live is constructed, there is always some delay between cause and effect, so sometimes your wishes can take a little while to manifest.

Although I don't know what happens scientifically to create the delay, I do know why the delay is essential. We don't always know what we want (even if we think we do), and we are frequently guilty of saying things we don't really mean. Have you ever said you wished someone would drop dead? Can you imagine the implications of that kind of request being answered instantly?

Lack of belief can also be a reason for delays in our wish manifesting in our life. Believe that your wish is truly possible, and it will happen. Remember that every single action you take, or thought you have, creates an effect like a Mexican wave, touching the lives of many people one by one and creating changes all around. It's a bit like dropping a pebble into a pond: the ripples start small, but can end up going a long way.

You can manifest joy and happiness in your life when you believe you can have them.

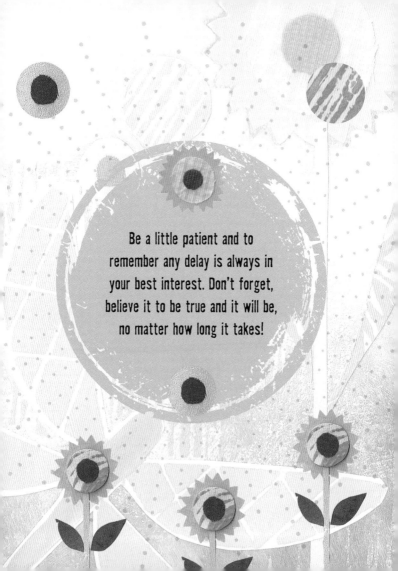

Be a little patient and to remember any delay is always in your best interest. Don't forget, believe it to be true and it will be, no matter how long it takes!

Visualize your dreams

Did you know that your brain cannot distinguish between thought and action? It triggers the same set of stimuli, whether you are thinking about something or actually doing it. That's why you can get excited thinking about something to such a degree that your heart races.

Visualizing your request happening is essential to the speed and accuracy of your manifestation. For example, if you wish for the holiday of a lifetime, follow this process:

- Imagine the white sand of the beach running through your fingers.

- Hear the sound of the waves on the shore, and your loved ones laughing near by.

- Let this "movie" run in your mind over and over again with increasing detail.

- Now visualize it and do a "dry run," or imaginary practice.

Athletes report greater success in races when they do this, visualizing their race beforehand. So step onto that plane, check into the hotel, swim, sunbathe... and manifest your dreams.

Make time to practice your dreams. Visualize what it will feel
like to get what you have asked for. There is no clearer
signal to the universe or your brain than a dry run!

Let the universe do its job

When we recognize the ways we impede our journey to happiness, we can negate them.

Often when there has been an absence of good things in our life, it's easier to believe that they won't come to us because we don't deserve them, or that happiness is something other people have. Another reason we veer off the path to our dreams is that sometimes we just can't see how what we really want can happen. Yet the universe can create miracles and has every possible option available to it, which we can't always foresee.

For example, recently I heard of funding for a new business coming not from a bank loan, but from a charity, an unexpected inheritance, and an unclaimed insurance payout—which made the new business owner's dream come true.

You don't have to know how your wish will be granted; you just have to believe that it will happen by having a bit of faith. Trust the limitless universe that can germinate seeds, bring perfect babies from a bunch of chromosomes, help night follow day follow night, and season follow season, to do its magic. Your dreams are no big deal for the universe. Just hand over your request and get on with your life, believing it will happen.

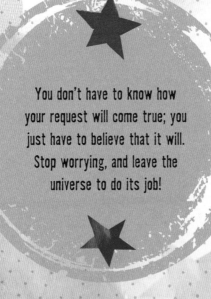

You don't have to know how your request will come true; you just have to believe that it will. Stop worrying, and leave the universe to do its job!

Let go of blame

Blame has to be one the most damaging and
restrictive emotions, stopping you from moving forward.
Sooner or later this pain, whether it is near to the surface
or deep inside you, will create far greater problems.

If you are blaming someone for hurting you, you are giving them
permission to control your life. No matter how traumatic the situation
that made you choose to blame, it is now in your past. It does not have
to affect your present or your future. This is not condoning bad
behavior or taking trauma lightly; it is about taking back your life and
letting go of the pain that your memories hold. The person who hurt
you will have to take responsibility for what happened within their own
life. No one is exempt from this, and although you may never get to
see things balanced out, you can guarantee they will be. All you
have to do is be willing (and I mean really willing) to let it go.

The second you say or feel that you want to stop blaming and take
responsibility for your life, the universe will act. People who can help
you heal will turn up. It is even possible that a situation may arise to
help you understand the viewpoint of the person who hurt you.

Release your past pain to the universe for it to be healed.
Identify where you place blame and let it go. It is
time for you to be free, whole, and happy again!

You can change your world in 16 seconds

Everything in the universe vibrates. The frequency of vibration determines how something looks, acts, and if we can perceive it. Generally, good emotions like love, joy, and happiness vibrate at a high frequency, whereas unpleasant things vibrate at low frequencies.

You can easily detect your own frequency, and the frequency of the things that are attracted to you, by how you feel. At the top end of the scale where pure love vibrates, there is happiness and off-the-scale joy. At the very bottom end, we find depression or complete shut-down. Ideally, we want to be vibrating way up there, feeling indescribable joy all the time.

To raise your frequency at will, recall a memory that feels good, for example:

- a baby laughing

- someone you love smiling at you

- being in your favorite place

- hearing your favorite song

Think a lot about what gets you so excited that you want to tell everyone—and you will feel your vibration shift a bit higher. Do something nice for yourself or someone else, and vibrate some more. Each time you raise your level, hold the feeling for 16 seconds—that's all it takes to raise your frequency and attract a better return.

When you ask the universe for something, ask from this "feelgood" place of your higher vibration. This strengthens your wish and helps it manifest.

Increase your vibration. Think of the things that make you smile and give them as much energy and time as you can until you start to feel joyful. Focus your energy on what you want for 16 seconds, and your dream will begin to manifest.

Take time out

So many of us these days have hectic lifestyles and
often head toward exhaustion and burnout as we try to meet
the unrealistic standards we set ourselves. It is easy to condone
the type of busy that earns us money or supports our families,
but often our workload can be counterproductive; certainly,
it can make connecting with the universe more difficult.

With so much being crammed into each day, taking time to recharge
our batteries can become almost impossible, and sleep alone won't
always do the trick. The most effective way to re-energize is to meditate.

Meditation is a great tool for all aspects of personal development. It can
help recharge energy levels and release stress, but also strengthen your
connection with the universe, advancing psychic development,

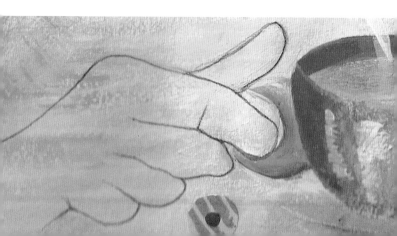

increasing your awareness and vibration, and promoting healing. This ancient practice will help you by ensuring that your request to the universe isn't impeded by tiredness or low energy.

Slow down and take time out to recharge your batteries. Try meditation to increase your energy levels and make a clearer connection with the universe. You'll feel better and be a giant step closer to your goal!

Find your happy place

The creative energy within the universe vibrates at a very high frequency. In order to effectively reach this force with your request, it is better to send it from a "feelgood' or "high–vibe" place.

Try any of these to help you reach a "feelgood" place:

- Imagine the face of someone you love.

- Think of an event or place that makes you happy.

- Remember something that made you laugh.

- Listen to a song that makes you want to dance and sing along.

The buzz you get from any joyful memories and thoughts like these pushes your vibration up the scale, and the more you buzz when you send your request, the more effective your request delivery will be. Also, simply being on your way to experiencing your dreams will make you feel even better still!

Pay attention to how you feel. If you learn to get yourself to a "feelgood" place and send out your request from there, success is guaranteed. Learn to feel good, and anything is possible!

Give thanks

Gratitude is essential in raising your vibration, particularly in the early days when connection to the universe feels like trial and error. But often we can forget to flow energy to the nice things that happen and spend hours concentrating on the state of the world and our bank accounts. Is there any wonder few of us feel joy?

Being mindful is an essential part of our evolution. Eastern philosophers and Buddhists have been pointing out the merits of mindfulness for centuries, yet here in the Western world we are just too busy to be mindful of the good things and say "thank you."

Set yourself a mental alarm clock. When someone does something nice for you, stop and acknowledge it. Say thank you like you mean it; your vibration will lift and the other person's will soar. Energy will flow to the good things in your life and, more importantly, you will become aware of the process. Don't forget to thank the universe, too, since this strengthens your connection, and abundance will flow to you.

When you concentrate on what you have, the things you don't have are put into perspective. When you think about those you share love with, you also automatically feel the higher vibration that goes with it and attract what you want into your life.

Acknowledge the abundance that you already have. Take time out where possible to recognize the good things that are already coming to you daily. Be grateful!

Where energy flows, energy goes

Energy makes everything happen. It determines how everything looks, acts, and moves. This spark of life, which fires every particle and wave in the universe, governs creation and gives matter its characteristics, depending on the wavelength or frequency at which it vibrates.

According to Einstein, energy cannot be destroyed, but changes its form. And as we are energy, this suggests that we too may change form and not be bound by physical laws. We might behave differently, but still exist.

Thoughts and beliefs are also governed by the flow of energy, and this thought-energy is worth monitoring. Whatever we concentrate on repeatedly, good or bad, will eventually manifest. Whether you are using your inner knowledge, belief system, thoughts, words, or actions, whatever you send out you will get back. Pay attention to where you are sending your energy:

- Is it going where you want it to go?

- Are your words, thoughts, and actions manifesting what you hope for?

- Are you in a joyful state of mind when you make your request?

- Will your request make you truly happy?

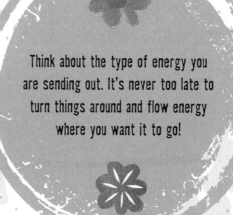

Think about the type of energy you are sending out. It's never too late to turn things around and flow energy where you want it to go!

Pay attention to how you feel and learn to read what your feelings are telling you. If you learn to understand them you can stay in a "feelgood" place most of the time, and manifesting all you desire will become as natural as breathing!

Pay attention to how you feel

It's common sense that feeling good is, well, good for us, but we often take our ability to feel for granted. Our feelings guide us through life; after all, an uneasy feeling in the pit of the stomach when something is wrong cannot be misread and will never let us down. Our feelings will always be honest with us and steer us in the right direction.

Much more of our intelligence comes from our heart and our gut than you might think; neurons responsible for thinking are abundantly present in the heart, and our gut secretes as much serotonin (happy hormone) as the brain. The heart sends more signals to the brain about what is going on in our being than vice versa, even though we would expect it to be the other way around.

Feelings also make life what it is. If we couldn't feel, the world would be a very empty place. This is because our feelings are a way to recognize, process, and understand the flow of life-giving energy that courses through everything in the universe, including us. We are able to perceive its presence because of our feelings. Paying attention to our feelings will lead us away from problems and guide us toward happiness and a frequency closer to that of the life we dream of.

Count your blessings

Gratitude is essential if we are going to keep our vibration high enough to manifest better things. It's good to send energy to our hopes and dreams, but concentrating habitually on what we already have will help keep things in perspective.

Life can be hectic, and in developed countries in particular, we often push ourselves really hard to achieve unreasonable goals and unattainable standards. This leaves next to no time for noticing the subtle blessings in our lives. You may think a great deal is wrong in your life if you don't take time to see just how much is, in fact, right. Look for the wonderful things people say and do for you. Count your blessings daily and see how much you already have. Be grateful and acknowledge your abundance, and your vibration will soar, bringing yet more gifts to you.

Try any of these ways to practice gratitude, and notice how they make you feel:

• Take time once a day to think about something you're grateful for—it could be a relationship, your home, your health, or something as simple as the smell of your coffee in the morning or the sun shining.

• Say thank you more to other people for the things they do for you and how much you appreciate them—whether it's your friends, family members, or colleagues.

• Keep a gratitude journal where once or twice a week you can write down several things you're grateful for and why.

Count your blessings. Spend time being aware of all you already have and allow your frequency to increase. Give thanks and expect the next instalment of your bounty.

Slow down and let the cosmos help you

The pace of life today can mean that we miss many opportunities to connect with the universe and flow energy in the direction we want it to go. Sometimes we let things get out of hand, and it's only when we find ourselves exhausted, lonely, or unhappy that we slow down and take stock.

To help you slow down, try incorporating a small dose of these things into each day:

- Count your blessings (see page 54).

- Do something you find fun.

- Rest and recharge.

- Show love to someone else.

- Laugh.

- Spend time on something that is important to you.

- Be mindful of the love others flow toward you.

The absence of these things will deplete us, and yet they can empower us, guarantee well-being, and give us the energy to get everything done. Take stock every day before you are so far down it takes a miracle to get back up.

Remember what is important.
Work and duty may be a priority when
bills have to be paid, but if you don't make
time to refuel your energy bank, you will
eventually grind to a halt. Enjoy yourself,
be grateful, and give and receive love today,
and you'll sail through everything else
that is less fun.

Check your progress

Every now and then it's good to check how things are going.
When you first begin practicing manifestation, write down your
wishes in the back of this book (see page 124) so you can tick
things off as they happen. This can also serve as an occasional
reminder of reasons to be grateful.

If in the beginning your request seems like a tall order (you may not
think a house in the country is easily attainable, for example), why
not place smaller things, like a bunch of flowers from an unexpected
source, on your list? To the universe, a bunch of flowers is no easier
to create than a Porsche, but if you believe it is, then a Porsche will
be more difficult to create. When the bunch of flowers arrives you will
begin to see that manifestation works, you will feel good because
flowers are lovely... and hopefully you will try for the Porsche!

Sometimes you might change your mind about what is important
and what to wish for, so a regular manifestation check-up gives
you the opportunity to re-evaluate.

Check the progress of your request, keeping it in mind
without panicking about the result. Frequent requests
to the universe and top-ups ensure your request
is really what you want when it arrives. Be grateful
as everything you hope for comes to you.

Unlock unresolved emotion

You may find it hard to believe that anyone would "choose" to be ill. Sometimes illness is part of our chosen path, but there is also a type of illness that we make for ourselves—illness we don't need to suffer through or have at all, which is created by leaving past traumas or emotionally based issues unresolved. It is the type that our stressful lives can help create, when there is no time for joy, and we are so busy that we forget to connect with our life force.

When in good health, the "life-giving energy force," or unconditional love (known as *chi* in China and *prana* in India) flows freely around the body. Hippocrates called it the *vis medicatrix naturae*, which means "the healing power of nature." Energy circulates via a system of energy pathways throughout the body adjoining the meridians. Sometimes when we are unable, or refuse, to let go of an emotionally-based issue, blockages are created that disrupt the flow of energy around the body.

Energy is our life force, and therefore if any area of the body cannot receive its quota, it will stop working properly, and illness will occur. Sooner or later this affects other parts of the body, too.

Recognize that there are two kinds of illness and do what you can to avoid the type you can create yourself. Identify where the blockages are; pinpoint the emotions, pain, and trauma that are unresolved and let them go. You can only reach your potential if you do this!

Have some fun

Children have the right idea about life because they know how to play. They know what makes them happy and how to have fun! It doesn't matter how little they have in the way of props—they can have fun anyhow.

We might tell ourselves that play is foolish or it's just for the kids, but having fun is essential not only to our well-being, but also to the manifestation process. Happiness, joy, and love are high vibrations. They fill us with life energy and make us feel alive! Remember, if something feels good, it is right for us, and it is meant to be and is part of our path. The universe attracts us to what we should be doing and having by dangling the "feelgood" carrot; it feels good because it is part of who we are. Feeling love, happiness, and joy is our natural intended state. When we feel joy we are in "divine flow."

Think about these free sources of joy and see how you are affected by the mere thought of them:

- a real belly laugh

- a genuine "I love you"

- a big, gummy smile from a baby

- a breeze on your face

- a cuddle (are you smiling yet?)

- a sunset

- a completed task

- a thank you
- a warm welcome
- giving gifts
- family
- a cat's purr
- the sea
- friendship
- a kiss

There are thousands more, but you get the idea. The key is to recognize what brings you joy. And when you know what it is, include it in your life every chance you get.

Remember the importance of having fun.
Damage occurs when our vibration drops too low, making the difference between the frequency of the life force and ours too great, stifling the flow toward us and through us. Any joy is guaranteed to raise our vibe. Remember to have fun and laugh when you can!

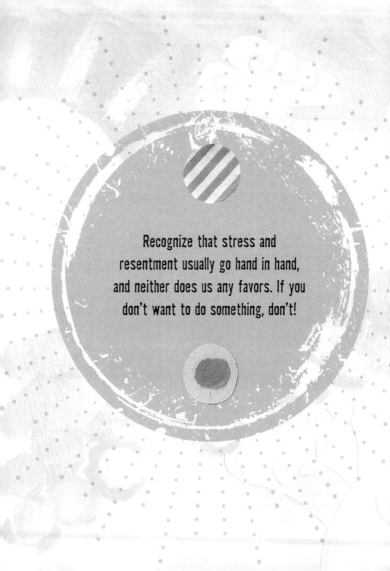

Recognize that stress and resentment usually go hand in hand, and neither does us any favors. If you don't want to do something, don't!

Say no sometimes

Nice people do stuff for others, don't they? Nice people act selflessly. Maybe so, but the act is negated if it's done because you think you have to do it, or because it is expected of you. In the realms of the universe, a good deed done under duress is pointless and has no karmic value whatsoever. If you are tying yourself in knots to help others and causing problems for yourself, it's also not a good thing to do.

Sometimes it is okay to say no and to put your own needs at the top of the list. This is not you being selfish. You are as important as anyone else within the universe. By all means, help your fellow man and spread unconditional love and joy where you can, but only do it if your heart is in it and your motive is genuinely to help, not just to look good.

Use these questions to help you decide whether to say yes or no:

- Am I saying yes just to fulfill others' expectations?

- Would saying yes deplete my time and energy?

- Does saying yes fit in with my own goals and values?

Balance is essential within the universe and is also essential for your own well-being. Give equal measures of love to yourself as well as everyone else.

Listen to what your body is saying and let it go

Our bodies were designed to last at least 140 years, yet there are very few that last anywhere near as long. This is because we generally live out of sync with the universe.

We hold all our sadness and anger inside, where it distorts and infects our bodies. We stay with pain, resentment, and unresolved emotional issues until they fester and become cancerous. We set ourselves impossible targets in life and suffer the stress of trying to attain them.

Aches and pains in our bodies give us a signal that there is a need to let go of unresolved emotional issues that continue to impede our health. For our bodies to heal, we need to release the trapped, "life-stripping" stuff. All we need to do is decide we want to feel better and pass the pain to the universe, so it can be dissolved into love, by love. We can affirm, set our intention, and blossom, but we also want to be able, physically, to reap the benefits.

With the help of the universe, you can heal every day by letting go of anything that blocks your access to the life you want. Hand it over to the universe and it will happen.

Release your pain and let the universe take care of it. You don't need to know how to heal your pain; you just have to want to be whole!

Intend to be well and happy

Intention is incredibly powerful! Nothing comes close to it. The force of intention was used to create everything there is; all that we can perceive and all that we can't. It is the force of creation. It goes without saying, then, that if we wish to recreate any part of our lives, we need to access the force of intention.

Understanding intention can be difficult. We are still too underdeveloped mentally and spiritually to grasp the whole concept, but we can definitely use intention to some degree. When we use intention, there are no grey areas; it is the language of the universe in its most fluent form. If you intend to do, or be, or have something, the universe gets a clear message that you really mean it and that you will participate, doing whatever you have to do to achieve your goal. Intention is determination and then some. Intention is so powerful that things start to move where you want them to the second you set the intention; sometimes that's all it takes.

Intention is put into action when you ask the universe to help you heal or let go of painful blame. It is the force that instigates the healing process without you having to do a thing other than intend to be healed.

Release the power you have within you. Use the power of your mind and set your intention for all that supports and nurtures your well-being!

Recognize what is right for you

Recognizing what is good for us is easy. Recognizing what we should be doing in this lifetime is also far less complicated than it might appear. The rules are generally that if it feels good, it is good, and if you're good at it you should be doing it.

Try not to complicate matters and lower your vibration in the process. It's okay to do fun stuff, enjoy what you do, and choose to do what you enjoy. The only barriers that prevent you doing just that are of your own making. If you need help jumping over, or even negating them, ask and it will happen!

Allow your vibration to rise every day. If something feels good, it is right for you and a clear signal that you are on the right path. Make time to enjoy yourself!

Forgive

One of the greatest tools in the healing process is forgiveness. If blame restricts and confines us, then forgiveness frees and liberates us.

We have all made mistakes in our lives; it is part of the learning process. You would not berate a small child for accidentally breaking something through curiosity or the clumsiness of his or her developing co-ordination. Yet many of us constantly beat ourselves up over past mistakes, so much so in some instances that we begin to believe that we are valueless. In some cases, it is not ourselves we are angry with, but someone else who has hurt us.

This is an even more harmful situation, leading to unresolved pain and trauma, but it can also lead to a lack of trust, not just with an individual, but with the entire human race.

To be free from either of these situations, we have to forgive, let go, and move on. If this were easy, very few of us would have to deal with ill-health or painful memories at all. It's not easy to do alone, but it's not impossible. For many, saying "I forgive you..." feels like giving a large part of ourselves to someone who doesn't deserve it. The easiest way to do this is to ask the universe to sort it for you. You don't need to know how, you just need to want to forgive and be free of the whole horrible mess once and for all. Forgiveness unlocks your potential, abundance, and happiness.

Forgive those who hurt you, and forgive yourself, too, if need be. Make space for joy to come into your life by offloading the pain!

Use the power of intention

Intention, the universal creative force, is put into action
when you are absolutely sure you know what you want.
It creates its magic when you have stopped the indecision
and you have well and truly made up your mind.

It is evident then that the most powerful creative force in the
universe is seriously inhibited by doubt and indecision. Worse still,
it can be blocked and rendered almost inactive by the notion that
we are separate from the rest of the universe.

To live the life we want, we have to remember who we are and decide
upon our direction in life. Usually, it is fear about making the wrong
choice that causes indecision. We can always adjust our intention
accordingly. If we look at any of the major breakthroughs, discoveries,
and inventions that our species has known, we can clearly see intention
at work. All the inventors, scientists, and explorers were fuelled by an
inner "knowing." They all persevered, sure that what they searched
for was possible. Never did they have the intention to prove that
something didn't exist or wasn't possible.

All the achievers of our time share the ability to visualize
something that is not yet solid. Our world is in a constant
state of becoming; nothing is fixed or concrete until we,
the observers, begin to perceive it.

Acknowledge that the force of
intention was used to create everything
there is. If we wish to work with the universe
to create any part of our lives, we can access
the force of intention. Use intention every
day, harness the creative forces of the
universe, and let your mind work for you.
The life you deserve is just a matter
of perception!

Be joyful

Most of the dreams and hopes you choose to manifest in your life usually have one motivation behind them—wanting to be happy.

You may know, or think you know, what will make you happy, which is fine; go ahead and manifest all you could hope for to come to you. But have you considered cutting out the middle man and going straight for the happiness?

When you request happiness, it will bring with it all the frills and thrills that you would probably ask for anyway. Voicing your request for happiness in the present tense speeds up its arrival. Try saying positive affirmations such as:

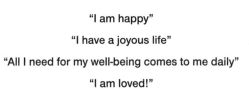

"I am happy"

"I have a joyous life"

"All I need for my well-being comes to me daily"

"I am loved!"

Recognize that happiness, joy, and love are high vibrations. Closer in frequency to creative energy, these vibrations fill you with life energy, making you feel alive. Feeling love, happiness, and joy is your natural intended state. When you feel joy, you are in "divine flow." Remember what makes you happy!

Embrace your life purpose

The life you live is down to you. Free will leaves us in control, but our chosen path is also governed by karma. We choose which karma to balance in each lifetime in the same way that we choose those who will help us along the way. There are no coincidences in life; people are always brought together at the right time to help with the task at hand, including karmic balance.

Karma can be instantaneous, but it can also take lifetimes to balance. Instant karmic balance happens when you project love onto someone and you immediately feel more loved. In contrast, when you project guilt onto someone, you feel guilty straight away, too. Sometimes you can't always tie the two ends of a transaction together because there is a period of time between the two.

Karma is not always about balancing debts, however. Karma can be a contract you have for spiritual growth while you are here. Yet at times, things don't feel balanced. If you have survived a barrage of loss, abuse, and adversity, you may feel you are being punished. Often, you have made a karmic contract to walk this path. You can learn so much about compassion, self-love, and inner strength due to this adversity and, as a result, speed forward spiritually.

Recognize that we were born with free will and choose how we live our lives. Recently, you may have been presented with a challenge. Acknowledging that karma is not punishment but a choice gives you a chance to grow spiritually. Know that your life purpose will include challenges, but it will always give you the opportunity to shine!

Love unconditionally

Unconditional love is, quite simply, love without exception. Nothing matters in the case of unconditional love except love itself. No condition can inhibit it because it is the love that the universe gives to us, no matter how many times we screw up.

Choice is part of unconditional love, as is freedom. When unconditional love is yours, you are given the freedom to be who you are, to make mistakes, and to still be totally loved. When we value something personally, we usually take care of it. It follows then that when we know we are loved, we realize how great we are, learn to love ourselves, and choose the right path, bringing happiness all round.

It is remarkable how amazing a person can become when loved unconditionally. Get into divine flow, the state of perfect resonance with the universe, and there is nothing that cannot be achieved.

Try saying these positive affirmations to help you show
unconditional love to yourself:

"I treat myself with kindness and compassion"

"I accept myself as I am unconditionally"

"I am resilient and strong"

"I love my body and everything that it does for me"

"I trust my decisions and believe in myself"

Unconditional love is one of the greatest gifts you can
give to anyone. Why not give this gift to yourself?

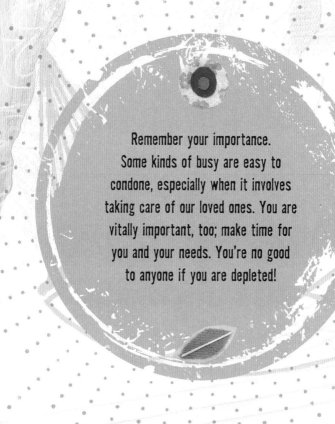

Remember your importance.
Some kinds of busy are easy to
condone, especially when it involves
taking care of our loved ones. You are
vitally important, too; make time for
you and your needs. You're no good
to anyone if you are depleted!

Make time for you

To achieve all that is expected of you and all that you expect of yourself, it is absolutely essential to make time just for you.

While we are all usually happy to take on the responsibility of caring for dependent loved ones, such as children or family members who are ill, sometimes guilt ensues if we don't do what we feel we should do in these cases—which is disabling and counterproductive to our well-being.

There doesn't have to be a choice between taking care of those who need you and taking care of yourself. You can, in fact, do both equally well without putting yourself second at all. Remember, you are more likely to get everything done if you are rested and happy in yourself.

Try any of these ways to make more time for yourself, even when you're busy:

- Ask for help when you need it from your family, friends, or colleagues.

- Do something you enjoy each day, whether that's reading, listening to a song, or taking a walk.

- Try to spend some time in nature each day—even if it's for as little as 5 minutes.

There is always hope

Sometimes, when we begin to manifest change, things get worse before they get better.

It's a bit like washing up: in the sink you put your dirty dishes (an unsatisfactory life), add hot water and washing-up liquid (affirmations and positive thoughts), and suddenly the water clouds with floating gunk and basically looks a bit of a mess. You have a choice at this point: give up and think that washing up doesn't work (after all, you have a worse mess now than you started with), or add more hot water and soap (positive thoughts and affirmations) and keep going.

Depending on how dirty your dishes are, or how far from being happy you are, sooner or later you will get a load of sparkly dishes. Eventually, any amount of mess will come clean.

No matter how bad things are now, they will get better eventually. Even if things seem to get worse in the beginning, remember the washing-up metaphor and keep going!

Now is important

Every moment, we have the opportunity to alter how we see our past and reprogram the future by changing how we live in the present. This particular moment, NOW, is the only moment that is important!

What we do and say and think at this point determines what we will experience next. It is what we believe in just now that has a real impact on our life.

Yet, despite this, we spend so much time concentrating on our past, and what we think about our past choices, actions, and experiences, especially if unpleasant, that it clouds the possibility of change.

Many of us can recall times we wish had been different. We often regret our actions, wishing we hadn't come into contact with someone who then hurt us, or we feel guilty about things said and done. Sometimes we want to omit entire chapters from our lives. Instead, try to recognize that the only moment that is relevant is this one and hand over the rest to the universe!

Be mindful of the present moment. The actions, thoughts, and feelings you are experiencing right now are busy creating what happens next. Forget the past. NOW is what counts!

It's all good

Nothing bad happens to us. It is how we react to experiences that creates the problems in our lives. The universe is always looking out for us, and everything we are presented with is always in our best interest and for the highest good.

- How many times have you worried about something, yet it turned out okay in the end?

- How many times have you tried to hold on to something you thought you wanted, causing pain all round, only to discover later that you were better off without it?

- Think about a difficulty or challenge you've faced—did it give you an opportunity to grow and learn?

- Has something that seemed like a failure ever redirected you to a new and better path?

With hindsight, it is easy to see that situations aren't always as they first appear. When presented with a challenge, go with the flow, armed with the knowledge that all will be well in the end. Life will be a lot easier. Maybe you could give it a try?

Look for the opportunity to grow within the challenges you may face. We can benefit from every situation; everything happens for the highest good, even if we can't see it initially.

A gift for you

Everything that happens to us unexpectedly will always steer us onto the safest path, even if we can't appreciate it at the time.

- Under every trauma there's a chance to grow.

- Behind every setback there's a chance to move forward in a better direction.

- Behind heartache there's a chance for new love.

- Endings are in fact beginnings, and everything happens in perfect order.

You may not recognize this until after the event, but rest assured one day you will! Trust the universe to show you the gift behind every challenge.

Try to see apparent problems as they really are. Don't let your fears take over, and look for the gift because there is always one!

It's no big deal

We can take life too seriously. Many of the things we worry about are really not important at all. There will still be things left undone when we pass over. There will still be cars to clean, shopping to do, bills to be paid, and work unfinished. None of it will worry any of us when we've moved on.

How many things that were all-consuming 10 years ago are still important or remotely relevant today? Not many! What may still be important to you are relationships that have stood the test of time, which is not at all surprising as we learn so much from them.

Try not to worry at all, but if you can't avoid worrying, keep everything in perspective; most things are just not a big deal. You probably can't remember what you worried about a month ago, let alone 10 years ago. You will survive the impact of leaving something behind if you have to, regardless of how crucial this situation might seem just now.

Try not to take things too seriously;
the things you worry about today
won't be as relevant tomorrow, and
in a week they will just be a memory.
All you can do is your best!

You are eternal

There are areas of our life in which we waste our creative energy, and fear takes over. As bigger wants hide behind other wants, bigger fears hide behind other fears. One of our greatest underlying fears, under so many more layers than you might think, is passing over.

Well, life doesn't end; our energy changes into another form of energy, and we continue to exist at another frequency. All we are doing here is training for what comes next. This life is a school where we train for the next dimension.

There is much more evidence, of both a scientific and spiritual nature, that we are eternal than there is evidence for this being all there is. Your belief system will influence how you react to this concept. Many times during my evenings of clairvoyance, a spirit will tell me they did not "believe" before they died; now they join the queue to validate their presence.

Acknowledge your divinity. You will live on, no matter what happens. You are so much more than this present body and life!

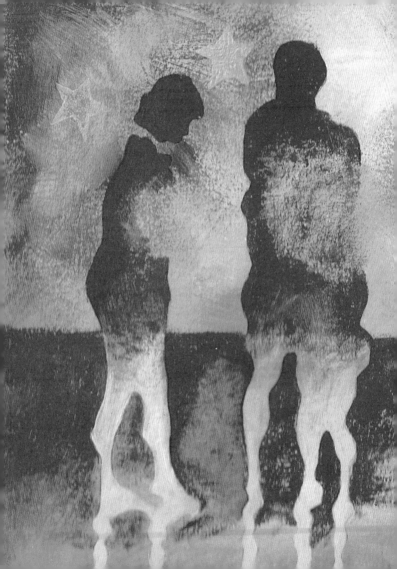

We will always have each other

We are incarnated in each lifetime with the same group
of souls. Maybe a different role is played out in each lifetime,
and a different relationship between the souls occurs,
but nevertheless the souls are still together.

- Death may separate us, but this is a temporary state,
  and we will always be reunited.

- Love cannot be destroyed—it simply changes to another
  frequency, and we take it with us.

- Like will still attract like, and similar energies will still
  be drawn together. We will be reunited again!

- Remember, we're all part of the whole: all linked
  together, and always will be.

Try not to worry about your loved ones. Should the worst
happen and you are parted, you will always be reunited with
the souls you value and love. You cannot lose someone for
good because they are part of you and you are part of them.

You can rewrite the ending

No matter what is happening in your life at this moment, you have the ability to change it. What you concentrate on will become real for you; your attitude governs what happens next.

Simply by focusing on the outcome you would prefer, strengthened by your beliefs and coming from a "feelgood" place, you can make a significant change to what is to come. Your past is irrelevant, and your future not yet determined. The only moment that is relevant is this one, and you are able to decide now what will happen next.

Generally, it is good to concentrate on being happy, and all results will support you in that. However, if something in life is particularly important to you, you can rewrite how it ends.

Remember that what you believe shapes your world. You can choose to believe anything you want; that's your prerogative.

It's all in the past

Life keeps changing, and as it ebbs and flows, the relevance of all situations will grow and diminish, but you are able to change the outcome of something by concentrating on it.

You can also use this ability to change how you see your past. Your past is no longer relevant, but if we have pain from the past we often hold on to it, especially if we didn't get the outcome we wanted. In this moment you can change the outcome of your past by letting it go, and the universe will tidy up all of the loose ends for you by helping you to understand what has happened and why.

You can rest assured that if there is a need for justice, it will happen. If you need closure, the universe will give you what you need, whether it's the chance to have your say, or the chance to see the situation for what it really is.

Let go of your past pain. Why not
choose to move forward instead?
Leave your past where it should be:
in the past. You don't have to
hurt any more.

It's not what you have but who you are

While we are busy manifesting the future we deserve and the exciting things that will make us happy, it is worth remembering one thing: we are not measured by our possessions.

We may look at the man with the beautiful home and his impressive Bentley on the drive, and feel he must be doing well and be happy. Yet we cannot be at all sure of this; invariably, wealthy, apparently successful people have the same ups and downs in life as those who struggle to make ends meet. There are happy rich people and there are happy poor people. The reason for this is that possessions come with happiness, not the other way around.

You can manifest anything into your life that brings you joy. Just remember that you are not measured by your possessions, job, home, and wealth. No one is!

Success comes with peace of mind, not the other way around.

Look fear in the face

The opposite of love is fear. Fear causes relentless
worry and can be completely disabling. To varying degrees,
the majority of us are terrified almost all of the time:
frightened of dying, of living, of making the wrong choices,
of being ridiculed, of not being good enough, of being alone,
of being dependant, and even of being happy in case
we have it taken away.

Most, if not all, fear is irrational. There may have been an initial
trigger, but generally any fear you have at this point is already out
of context and far greater than it needs to be. You can rest assured
that even if your fear at one time seemed justified, this is definitely
no longer the case. Fear keeps us from love, from life, and from
ever raising our vibe higher than a minor buzz.

If we take time to look at our fears and try to understand them, they
will more than likely disappear. Happiness is our natural state, and
that's why we want it. It is the nearest we can get in this physical
form to being pure spirit. It makes us feel alive and aware of the
life force within us. Being unhappy has the opposite effect, as
we feel dead and detached from the life force, and anything
that may cause this is what all our fears are based upon.
Acknowledge this, and you dissolve the fear.

Remember that your fears aren't real. All you are really frightened of is not feeling alive or happy. Instead of concentrating on your fears, which guarantees to move you away from feeling happy and alive, why not concentrate on something that makes you buzz? Seeing your fear for what it really is will put it in perspective.

You have a magic mirror— ask it to grant your wish

At every point in our lives we attract what we need to support our future development. We also attract those who reflect us just as we are. If we are sending out love, we will see love in the faces of those around us; if not, we won't.

When our vibrations match those of someone else, we become aware of each other. We magnetize similar people in similar circumstances to our own. We also attract those who confirm what we believe to be true. This is great if we are surrounded by loving, supportive people, but sometimes you might find that the opposite is happening. It can be very difficult to take responsibility for this by looking at what you are presented with daily from others, seeing your part in it, and asking how you can change it.

If you find yourself in a confrontational situation, ask what you are bringing to it. Are you tired and irritable? Angry? Frightened? Are these emotions relevant, or is there another reason for them? Perhaps you have other real worries on your mind and cannot deal with anything else. All these factors might contribute to you acting defensively. To turn the situation around, offer a loving way forward. You are not giving up your power, just putting yourself in a more productive position, with the unconditional backing of the universe. What you send out to others also affects you!

See your behavior reflected back to you. You attract the people and circumstances you need to develop as a person, along with those who act as mirrors, offering you a picture of exactly where you are right now. Give out love, and you will see this love reflected in the faces of everyone around you.

It's all relative

Relationships are as essential to our development as our connection to the universe. They give us the best conditions in which to learn. Where else can you see the result of an action without having to take the action yourself?

Even though this is the case, we rarely emerge from any relationship unscathed. Even when we mean well, we spend far too much time and energy trying to change and manipulate things or people to fit in with how we think they should be. We try to control, but control is nothing to do with unconditional love. Someone nearly always gets hurt, and it's exhausting! A lot of the problems that occur can be avoided if we realize control is never going to create a perfect relationship. The only things we have control over are our own lives and choices.

We could have a much easier time if we gave up trying to steal the energy we need from each other and found our own happiness, instead of being disappointed when others can't create that for us. With the help of the universe, we can fill our lives with everything that we want and need. We can share it with each other and give the best we have and have the best others can give—without trying to change anyone in the process.

Remember the importance of your relationships with others. Through each other, we learn about love and acceptance and find opportunities to make changes.

Crank up the volume

We often take sound for granted, yet it is essential for our health, well-being, and spiritual development. As with words, sound can make a significant impact. Sound can break through energy blockages, travel across the universe, alter our frequency, and help us reach our spiritual potential.

Sometimes we hear but don't listen. Listening is really about heightened perception. It's about taking the processed data and giving it your attention; acknowledging the feelings that a sound may have evoked and finding out

what they mean to you. If you don't really listen to sound it becomes merely noise. Paying attention to it allows you to transcend the noise and connect or resonate with the vibration.

According to ancient Chinese wisdom, music is one of the basic means of improving and refining human life, and it is clear to see that music means something to us all; it makes us want to move and dance, and can amplify and even change how we feel. On a challenging day, listening to uplifting music can change the direction our day is heading. Play music that makes you feel good, and you will stay in the right frequency for good things to come your way!

Make use of the greatest tool for frequency–boosting: music! Let music make you feel good.

Sing along

Music is not only a great tool for frequency–boosting, but also a great joy! If we sing along to music, the sounds we make with our voices vibrate in our heads. We then increase the effect of the music as we begin to vibrate from inside out as well as outside in. Coupled with the power of the lyrics, we can alter how we feel.

Humming or singing along to any sound will help you resonate with it, which is how sound facilitates change. When two vibrations of a similar frequency meet, as with the entanglement of atoms, they merge and become the same. This is called "entrainment," brought about by nature's need to be as efficient as possible. It is efficient for two vibrations to merge because less energy is used in co-operation than in opposition. If you hum or sing while listening to a sound and allow yourself to really perceive it, your whole body will resound in unity.

Take the benefits of sound and music one step further. Singing along to uplifting music allows it to affect your frequency from the inside as well as outside. Depending on its frequency, sound that you resonate with can lift a low vibration and re-attune you to a higher level.

Harness the powerful effects of sound and vibrations: hum or sing along to joyful music, and notice how it changes the way you feel.

What's the truth?

Did you know that your thoughts don't always tell you the truth? They can often tell you that you need to worry and something bad may happen. Yet you can never really know for certain what will happen because things change constantly.

There are so many influences that could come into play at any moment to change things. The more you worry or fix your energy on the possible problem, the more chance there is of it happening.

Try any of these ways to help you challenge anxious thoughts:

• When worries occur to you, write them down on a piece of paper and set aside a short amount of time to come back to them later—this allows you to get distance from negative thoughts, helping them to lose their power.

• Think about what you would say to a friend who was having the same worry.

• Is there any evidence that your negative thought is true? Is there a more positive way of looking at the situation?

You cannot know what the truth is for tomorrow, so don't listen to the unqualified fibs your thoughts might tell you. The only moment you can truthfully know about is this one!

Pay attention to your thoughts.
Are you being honest with yourself?
Always ask yourself if your thoughts
are telling you the truth.

Recognize your ego

Ego is fundamentally a sense of self. If you sometimes measure yourself according to what is going on in your life, where you live, how you behave, and what possessions you have, your ego is at work.

It encourages you to occasionally feel superior, and frequently inferior, but never equal. It feeds your fears. It drives you to want more things in search of a buzz, yet spend less time on what really makes you happy. It has a warped sense of value; its priority list has money and status at the top, and love for each other at the bottom. It promotes overworking for poor wages, leading you to believe that is all you are worth.

As love is within us all, ego is present within us too. So why do we have it when it causes so much pain? It is within us because balance is essential to live this life. We need the yin and yang, the dark and light, the love and fear, and every other opposite that exists. Without opposites, free will cannot exist in the fullest sense. There would never be anything other than good choices to make, so we would learn nothing, and we would give up as if someone else were making all our decisions. Our ego gives us choices, as does the love within us, but ultimately it is our free will that gives us the control to decide which way to go.

Pay attention to your ego, but then believe the opposite of what it tells you. Your ego will encourage you to veer off your path and away from your dreams. Your ego will tell you none of these messages from the universe works and that there is no hope! Your higher self knows better. If it feels good, it is right for you. If it doesn't feel good, it's probably your ego at work.

Recognize when you are in victim mode
and know you can be free of it. Victims
believe that bad stuff always happens to them
and usually they get what they ask for. After
a trauma, make the choice to stop hurting and
choose to believe that you are doing better,
and that good things are coming to you.
What you believe to be true will be!

Don't be a victim

There are times when we all behave like victims, such as when our ego takes over and we lapse into a victim mentality.

Victims are people who believe that they have no control over their lives, and they like to spend time concentrating on what is wrong. Victims live in the hope that tomorrow will be better, but never pay attention to what is good about today. They believe they have to graft for a living and are probably in dead-end jobs, earning next to no money. Their relationships are difficult, they feel like the laws of the universe don't apply to them, and they will deliberately choose the opposite of all the guidance within this book and others like it. Victims are scared of change and terrified of being disappointed, so prefer to stay in a bad place; they even look for the ulterior motive in every good thing that happens to them.

We all have days when we feel like giving in and having a good old moan, and sometimes that is therapeutic, but victims will always want anyone who will listen to know how bad they think things are for them, constantly fuelling the negativity by giving it all their energy.

Five joys a day

If variety is the spice of life, and joy is essential to our well-being, why not make a habit of incorporating five pieces of joy a day into your life? Whatever it is that makes you happy, include it in your daily routine.

- If you drink coffee, buy the best you can afford.

- If you like dancing, dance whenever you get the opportunity to do so.

- If you like to sing, whether you're good at it or not, sing!

- If you enjoy cooking, prepare yourself a delicious meal and take the time to sit down and savor it without distractions.

- If you want to exercise, choose an activity that you really enjoy—whether it's swimming, running, or yoga.

Whatever joys work for you, have at least five of them every day. They will help to keep the less-than-joyous duties in perspective, raise your vibrational frequency, and speed you toward the life you deserve!

Treat yourself well. Make a promise to yourself that you
will find at least five pieces of joy and incorporate them
into your day. If it makes you smile, have it and do it,
and your vibration will increase!

Offer love then leave it

There is a pitfall when we love someone—that is, the danger of getting too involved in their stuff! If someone close is worrying about something, be careful because often we want to try to fix it.

Helping others is natural when you understand how connected we all are, but getting too involved is counterproductive and can lead us straight into victim mode. Apart from giving them all our money and tiring ourselves out, we could be preventing them from learning something they need to know or fulfilling a karmic obligation. So how far do we go when someone we love is hurting?

Asking the person what they need is an obvious first step, but it is one we usually omit, especially with young people. Instead of asking, we usually go straight to fixing the problem. This is not useful at all; they are dealing with their mistake, karma, lesson, or choice, not ours. No matter how much we want to spare them the pain, they need to sort it out by themselves to find the gift behind the trauma. We cannot know just what they have chosen to look at in this lifetime, and we cannot know that our help is, in fact, helpful.

Avoid draining yourself and others by interfering in their lives. How do you truly help someone you love? The answer is to let them guide you, instead of thinking you know what they need. Ask them what you can do to help, be there for them, but don't try to fix it. You can be too involved in other people's lives. Remember, if you can't do anything about it, it's not about you!

Your list of wishes

Use these pages to write down your requests,
and then tick off each one as it happens.

....

....

....

....

....

....

....

....

....

....

....

....

....

....

....

....

....

....

....

....

....

....

....